WESTERN EROTICA HO

Also by Bram Riddlebarger:

Messages From the American Trashcan (Cabal Books, 2020)
Poem 3A.M. (Nihilism Revised, 2019)
Golden Rod (Cabal Books, 2018)
Earplugs (Livingston Press, 2012)
The Wheelhouse (Dead Bait 4 Anthology, Severed Press, 2017)
Chez Filthy (JK Publishing, 2009)

WESTERN EROTICA HO

a poetic attempt on vacation

by Bram Riddlebarger

Trident Press
Boulder, CO

Copyright © 2020 Bram Riddlebarger

Without limiting the rights under copyright, no part of this publication may be reproduced, stored in or introduced into a retrieval system, or transmitted, in any form or by any means (electronic, mechanical, photocopying, recording, or otherwise), without the prior written permission of both the copyright owner and the publisher of this book.

ISBN: 978-1-951226-06-0

Edited and typeset by Taylor Sumner
Cover art by Samuel Colosimo

Published by Trident Press
940 Pearl St.
Boulder, CO 80302
tridentcafe.com/trident-press

for the Lewis River Bear, keep running

Contents

1. I

Driving Your Guts Out
Zen and the Art of Climbing a Motorcycle in
   Cedar Rapids, Iowa
Traffic Sign Name, Minnesota
Athens, Ohio, to Badlands
   National Park, South Dakota, Part I
Middle of America, to Badlands National Park,
   South Dakota, Part II

8. II

Cedar Pass Campground, Badlands, South Dakota
Moon Over the Badlands

In the Dark Church of Commerce at Wall Drug,
    South Dakota
Black Hills, South Dakota
Rod and Gun Campground
Interrupted Thought
Morning
Onion Sandwich in Gillette, Wyoming
Windshield Laundromat
Campfire Traveler
Latrine Camper
Nola
Laundromat Fishing
Thermopolis, Wyoming
Journey into Yellowstone National Clusterfuck

Untitled
Teeth Bikinis
Old Faithful
Lewis River Bear
William Faulkner's Porch
I'm Just Going Through the Motions
Hot Dogs for Dinner with Black Beans
    and Dale's Pale Ale

Teton

Glance Affair

Shoshone National Forest Wilderness Area
  at Roaring Fork Lake

Lemon

S., My Star

Pleiades

The White Tombstones of Rawlins, Wyoming

39. III

Spoon

Jeffrey City, Wyoming

Blocks

On The Edge of Medicine Bow National Park

The Luxury Diner

47. IV

The End of Our Camping Journey

Where the Corn Does Not Grow

Gobble Across America

Bovine S'mores

Fort Kearney, Nebraska

Omaha, Nebraska

Future

Hotel Bed in Omaha

Midwest Greeting

Water to Wind Via Concrete

Popping Buttons in Peoria, Illinois

Bubbles

I

Driving Your Guts Out
8-4-12

After driving all night long,
as the mosquitoes squash
like hours
onto the windshield,

in the morning,
as the sun
rises
again,

the cars swarm
in packs
back
onto the hot pavement.

Zen and the Art of Climbing a Motorcycle in Cedar Rapids, Iowa
8-4-12

Round, little motorcycle man
with heavy motorcycle boots,
your look of Olympic determination,
as you kick a straight leg—
thump!—

up and onto your motorcycle seat.
You pause here,
gathering up
will on one leg like
a leather-clad flamingo,

like a do-rag heavy metal ballerino
with one heavy boot
on the barre,
then,
as an orb follows a parabola,

you slide—
success!—
across your saddle.
Onward
to Sturgis.

Traffic Sign Name, Minnesota
8-5-12

Kiester
Wells,

O,
the things

you would do
if

you were
real

and not
just

two places
on a sign

somewhere
in Minnesota.

Athens, Ohio
to Badlands National Park, South Dakota
Part I
8-5-12

Motorcycle
parade
to
Sturgis,
97°
annoying.

Middle of America
to Badlands National Park, South Dakota
Part II
8-5-12

1,200
miles
of
motorcycles
making
noise.

II

Cedar Pass Campground
Badlands, South Dakota
8-5-12

We
are
all
here
in
this
campground,
like
pimples
on
an
old face.

Moon Over the Badlands
8-5-12

I hope
that
I do not
have to pee tonight,

because there are
too many
people
in this camp.

In the Dark Church of Commerce at Wall Drug, South Dakota
8-6-12

There is no one in
the Traveler's Chapel.

Everyone is everywhere
else

looking for
five cent coffee

in the dark
church of commerce

at Wall Drug,
South Dakota.

Black Hills, South Dakota
8-6-12

Black Hills in early August,
the motorcycles of Sturgis
swarm like black flies,

like black visions

of a monster

that has stolen

our future.

Rod and Gun Campground
8-6-12

My three children:
ages nine,

seven,
and one,

louder
than motorcycles

in this
camp.

Interrupted Thought
8-6-12

Interrupted thought,
you

were going to criticize
me,

but I wish
that

we were making
love instead.

Morning
8-7-12

I ran four short miles
in the Black Hills

of South Dakota,
after fighting late at night

with S.
about kids, lack of sleep,

and too many miles
on the road.

The run
was okay, but

I could not see
anything sacred,

because
I was still drunk.

Onion Sandwich in Gillette, Wyoming
8-7-12

Onion sandwich
in Gillette, Wyoming,

you tasted so good
that I could still taste you

100 miles later,
as the Bighorn Mountains

spread like an unoccupied smile
in front of me.

Windshield Laundromat
8-7-12

Poor little notebook,
you were almost ruined last night
in the tent,
drenched with water

in the Black Hills
of South Dakota,
by a clumsily unfastened
water bottle lid.

Thank you
for drying out today
on the dashboard
of our car.

Campfire Traveler
8-7-12

The scout badge
of smoke.

Latrine Camper
8-7-12

The scout badge
of pit
toilet stink.

Nola
8-8-12

He was born
with a giant carrot

in his mouth.
This carrot

caused hysterics
among many

of the women.
These are

the stories
told late

at night
around campfires

in Western
America.

Laundromat Fishing
for M.
8-8-12

Inside
the silver

sud drum,
her

red
pocket knife

leaps around
like a fish.

Thermopolis, Wyoming
8-8-12

It took
a long time

to get here,
like 1000

year-old
eggs

rotting
into

a warm
embrace.

Journey into Yellowstone National Clusterfuck
8-8-12

Watch
out

for bears,
and be sure

to bring
your people spray.

8-9-12

Blank,
forgotten
page
in
this
notebook,
your
wit
should
reconcile
my
life.

Teeth Bikinis
8-8-12

If you look closely
in Yellowstone National Park,

you will see that all the rocks have claws
and that all the trees have teeth.

The purported bears, however,
do not exist,

and the bison are sunning
in bikinis.

Old Faithful
8-8-12

We waited eighty-three minutes
to see you erupt your caldera steam

up and into the hot August sun.
But like jealous lovers,

we did not stick around
to witness your final thrust.

Lewis River Bear
8-8-12

I was
so excited

to see you,
my first bear,

that I put my
cowboy hat

on backwards,
jumped

from the car,
and

ran to you
like a fly

to fresh
shit.

William Faulkner's Porch
8-9-12

This campground
at Lizard Creek would
not suit Bill Faulkner.
When I awoke in my
blue tent at 4am,

I had to sneak
out and crouch
and surreptitiously pee
off the frontporch dirt—
ah!—

surrounded by sleeping
eyes
like a densely-populated,
fictional county
somewhere in Wyoming.

I'm Just Going Through the Motions
8-9-12

I am just going
through the motions

of this vacation,
like a vacation actor

who is no longer
on the set.

Hot Dogs for Dinner with Black Beans and Dale's Pale Ale
8-9-12

We hiked around String Lake,
Grand Teton National Forest,
and up Paintbrush Canyon a bit.
Then bathed in String Lake:
a pretty nice bathtub.

The kids just kept screaming.
Later, at dinnertime,
a mule deer fawn ran into our camp,
and, startled by our blue tent,
it stopped.

"Have a Dale's," I said.
"And maybe a hot dog, too."
"I'm not old enough to drink,"
said the fawn. "Although, soon,
I will be old enough to shoot,

like an inaccurate memory
of the Vietnam War."
I took a bite of black beans then
that looked like everything
that a mule deer would ever leave.

Teton
8-9-12

How I wished
I could cup

your breast,
as my body

penetrated the cool
glacial water

of String Lake
when I was dirty,

like pencil lead
washing from under

my skin,
like snow

melting
into now.

Glance Affair
8-11-12 am

That look between you two
was like an orgasm of fire

dancing down
the long thin

monogamous thread
of our relationship,

burning the hillsides of our love
like the charred

and ruined hills
of Yellowstone.

Shoshone National Forest Wilderness Area
at Roaring Fork Lake
8-11-12

Shoshone National Forest Wilderness Area
at Roaring Fork Lake,

you hold no fish.
Our forks will be silent

tonight.
Our bellies will roar.

Goddamn trout, you are
jumping too far out.

It is awfully
pretty though,

like the landscape
of an empty plate.

Lemon
8-11-12

We held hands coming
down from the lake
in the mountains of Wyoming.
We had not caught any fish.

Scrubby pines
held our other hands
the whole way down to camp,
where we fried zucchini

and potatoes in foil
over a campfire.
The lemon we had bought for our trout
instead became a yellow dinosaur

resting beside a lake
high in the mountains of Wyoming
intent on extinction
like love without feeling.

S., My Star
8-11-12

Although
there are

millions of stars
overhead,

I will
concentrate

on just one,
and that is you.

Pleiades
8-12-12

We watched the Pleiades
last night burn through
the 10,000 ft. mountain sky
of Wyoming, outside Lander,
in Shoshone National Forest.

We met a man named Zahn
and a man from Ft. Worth, Texas,
via Michigan, whose wife
had an inner ear condition
that resulted in occasional

drunken bouts of wandering.
Now, we are off the mountain and driving
through the vast sage plains
of interior Wyoming,
heading to Rawlins to resupply

for one more camp
before hotels to Ohio.
The Olympic Games close
along with our journey
to the West with our kids.
Tails of fire burn out.

The White Tombstones of Rawlins, Wyoming
8-12-12

White tombstones
just off the road

in Rawlins, Wyoming,
alone

in the vast space
of open country,

which we had driven
for days.

Penitentiary markers
of old,

there was not
enough room

out there
for everyone.

III

Spoon
8-12-12

Sage plant, fill my nostrils
like the warm curl

of a lover's back,
nestled together

under the stars
of a 10,000 ft. mountain,

counting
the Pleiades,

as they spill
across the heavens

above prayers
like you.

Jeffrey City, Wyoming
8-12-12

Jeffrey City, Wyoming,
almost a ghost town,
right there as we drove past.
Even the liquor store
had closed.

Only one bar remained
for Taco Tuesdays.
No churches in sight.
Tenant housing: boarded up.
Sage plants played

every position on the baseball
diamond. The chain-link backstop
now shade for a small cow
chewing plug.
The Top Hat Motel sign

faded
to permanent vacancy.
The whole town looked almost
like the barren
sage plains again.

Blocks
8-12-12

We are camped in Vedauwoo Campground
between Laramie and Cheyenne, Wyoming.

Interstate 80 grinds away
not far and in sight

just up the rocks.
Here close to Happy Jack Road

the rocks are like
a baby Titan's wooden blocks

in which chipmunks run amok
and flies buzz

and the wind does not remember
which way it should blow,

and so it changes constantly,
confused by the rocks.

We eat the remainder of our road food:
a can of clam chowder mixed with water,

buns grilled in foil with cheese and onion,

potatoes under a can of baked beans with Tabasco

and mustard,
foil-steamed sweet onion,

one bottle of beer,
2 drinks each of whiskey,

and s'mores.
The sun sets, and we will rise early.

Back east toward Omaha for a night.
500 miles of interstate and Nebraska plains.

On the Edge of Medicine Bow National Park
8-12-12

We have not heard a coyote
in over a week. Their mouths
are too dry from this hot summer.
Perhaps they croak like frogs
on the edge of the dry rivers

and evaporated lakes.
The cars and the people buzz,
like drought-tolerant mosquitoes.
They yammer like children.
Coyote tongues cannot reach them.

Our fire ring smolders, as do our brains,
cooked on weeks of respite-less camping.
Nothing but the beauty of the land
and the relentless pressure
of close quarters.

The Luxury Diner
8-13-12 am

We picked the Luxury Diner
in Cheyenne, Wyoming, for breakfast:
the kids ate silver dollar pancakes,
while our youngest drank complimentary apple juice
from a cruddy high chair

in this converted railcar establishment.
We ordered breakfast burritos
covered in canned green chili.
The coffee, O, weak but needed
after a pre-dawn start from camp

and fifty miles of driving.
Our tongue-pierced waitress
arrived just after us, then waited
and served us well.
The two cooks laughed

slinging eggs
in the open kitchen.
The Western locals shot the shit,
as they must always do,
beside the claustrophobic bathroom.

This was the right

wrong side of the tracks.
A true vignette.
Thank you,
Luxury Diner.

IV

The End of Our Camping Journey
8-13-12

Good-bye,
pit toilets.

Where the Corn Does Not Grow
8-13-12

Western Nebraska, I think
that you are pretty.

But I wish that
I were walking across you

after
the Apocalypse

and that I was carrying
plenty of water.

Gobble Across America
8-13-12

Nebraska turkey,
strutting along a fence

beside the interstate,
you were headed west,

as we throttled east.
I do not think

that you will ever see
the mountains of Wyoming

at the rate
that you are going.

Bovine S'mores
8-13-12

The hay bales lie
under the big Nebraska
sky
like dun-colored
marshmallows

that only cattle
will eat
from the dry fields
beside
the corn rows

and not in a camp
around a cold fire
with graham crackers
and squares
of chocolate.

Fort Kearney, Nebraska
8-13-12

The inside
of Fort Kearny
is empty.

Everything in there
must still
be under the grass.

Omaha, Nebraska
8-13-12

If a heart
beat

like a pulse
at the periphery

of a rainbow,
you

would be
a pot of gold.

Future
8-13-12

Peoria, Illinois,
what do you hold?

Your name
evokes bad smells.

Your Mark Twain Hotel
holds fathoms of intrigue.

Your setting
along the Illinois River,

buzzing past,
half asleep at 3am

on our ride
out West

caught my fancy.
Now,

you are the future.
We will be there soon.

Hotel Bed in Omaha
8-14-12

Hotel bed in Omaha,
your sheets
are a butcher's apron of words.
Your blanket

is a knife that cuts me out.
Waking at 3am alone,
I am only covered
with remorse.

Midwest Greeting
8-14-12

Driving
back into Iowa,

every single tassel of corn
waves hello.

Water to Wind via Concrete
8-14-12

Giant wind turbine rotors
like white whales
strapped to the beds of semi-trucks

continue to pass by us
heading west, as we
head east.

They must swim up
from the Gulf of Mexico
and beach themselves

along the Mississippi,
far from the wrath
of Ahab,

and wait
for the trucks to carry them,
spinning, to a new blue.

Popping Buttons in Peoria, Illinois
8-14-12

We drove up
to the Peoria Heights Tower,

after dinner
at Peoria Hofbrau.

From the wonderful
vantage

of the tower,
we looked out

over the bluff,
stretching toward home,

over
the Haves

to where the Have-nots
eat so well.

Bubbles
8-15-12

The words on this page
are the soap bubbles
from a child's pink wand.
They are thoughts of home,
shimmering in the wind,
then gone like the end
of a long journey.

OTHER VERY FINE TITLES FROM
TRIDENT PRESS

Blood-Soaked Buddha/Hard Earth Pascal
by Noah Cicero

Marking a significant departure from Cicero's fictional and poetic works, *Blood-Soaked Buddha/Hard Earth Pascal* is a lucid philosophical treatise. Rather than entertain dogma, Cicero approaches a discussion of Buddhism from the refreshing perspective of the everyman, providing a profound spiritual analysis as well as a sharp critique of capitalism. There are even some pretty good ghost stories.

it gets cold
by jasper avery

it gets cold demands a body that is both the haunting and the house, a queerness that is both living and dying. What can be gained by inhabiting this liminal space? What can the inhabitation of dying bring to the living? What can be done when it gets cold?

Major Diamonds Nights & Knives
by Katie Foster

Major Diamonds Nights & Knives is a poetry project modeled after a deck of cards. While writing this poem, Katie Foster felt possessed by a spirit who died in childbirth. She tried to tell her story as best she could.

Cactus
by Nathaniel Kennon Perkins

"Shades of Updike's 'A&P' but much less boring." - Bart Schaneman, author of *The Silence is the Noise*

"Perkins does what classic literature does. He invites you to witness an accident, and like the desert, it is beautiful."
- Noah Cicero, author of *Nature Documentary*

Sixty Tattoos I Secretly Gave Myself at Work
by Tanner Ballengee

Ex-girlfriends. LSD. Motorcycle and canoe trips. *Sienfeld*. Skateboarding. Drunk friends and punk rock and shitty jobs. *Sixty Tattoos I Secretly Gave Myself at Work* is the most beautiful, the most vulnerable of punk and adventure memoirs. Each vignette centers around a hand-poked tattoo that the author gave himself on company time.

The Pocket Peter Kropotkin

Collected in this cute, pocket-sized volume are eight of Kropotkin's essays. The book starts with his indispensable article on anarchism, originally written for the Eleventh Edition of the *Encyclopedia Britannica*, and moves forward to expound on his ideas, which include prison abolition, syndicalism, expropriation, etc.

The Pocket Emma Goldman

Some great Goldman essays collected in one place. This book is perfect for carrying in your pocket so you can secretly read anarcha-feminist literature while you're supposed to be working.

The Silence is the Noise
by Bart Schaneman

After a few years living in cities, Ethan Thomas returns to his rural Nebraska hometown and takes a reporting job at the community newspaper. He stumbles upon a big story when an out-of-state oil company pumps enough fracking wastewater into the ground to induce earthquakes. As Ethan learns to write he reconnects with a young woman from his childhood. This is a story about the complicated relationship we have with the places we know best, the pull of the outside world, and finding something to love.

The Pocket Aleister Crowley

Famously called "the most evil man in Britain," Aleister Crowley's impact upon the occult tradition was nothing short of monumental. The selected works contained within this pocket-sized volume offer a way of thinking that is scientific and individualistic, but also deeply mythic and metaphysical, leaving room for both human intelligence and religious inspiration.

Propaganda of the Deed:
The Pocket Alexander Berkman

It was July 23, 1892, and Alexander Berkman was planning to die. He just had some business to attend to first. Dressed in a new suit and a black derby hat, Berkman burst into the Pittsburg office of Henry Clay Frick, the notoriously anti-union manager of the Carnegie Steel Company. From his pocket, Berkman produced a pistol.

This pocket-sized book collects the shorter works of one of the world's most influential anarchists.

The Soul of Man Under Socialism
by Oscar Wilde

"Socialism, Communism, or whatever one chooses to call it, by converting pricate property into public wealth, and substituting co-operation for competition, will restore society to its proper condition of a thoroughly healthy organism, and insure the material well-being of each member of the community."

Los Espiritus
by Josh Hyde

Four grandmas stop the passing of generational karma by interrupting a wedding with a funeral. Los Espiritus is an absurdist, spiritual romantic comedy with a heartfelt message: "How do we transcend our humanity?"

America At Play
by Mathis Svalina

America At Play is a collection of instructions for children's games. Part poetry, part whimsy, part despair, games such as "Freight Train Tag,""Baptism," & "World War" teach valuable lessons, such as how to play & how to be American. It is, Heraclitus said, reality's nature to remain hidden, but its rules are easily observed.

The Pocket Austin Osman Spare

Working on the cutting edge of both magic and art, Austin Osman Spare developed a unique synthesis of older ritual magic systems with post-modern, erotic, and surrealist themes. His theory of magic eschews complex formula and ritual to favor creativity, spontaneity, and ecstasy, embracing artistic expression and alternative sexualities. Collected here are some

With a Difference
by Francis Daulerio and Nick Gregorio

Cowritten by poet Francis Daulerio and fiction writer Nick Gregorio, With a Difference is inspired in part by Rancid and NoFX's 2002 BYO split cover album. Gregorio has adapted ten of Daulerio's poems into stories, and Daulerio has turned ten of Gregorio's stories into poems. Like a vinyl record, the book must be flipped over to read both "sides."

https://www.tridentcafe.com/trident-press